MASTERING THE ART OF PROFESSIONAL LOVE

S. A. KRISHNA BHARATHI

Copyright © S. A. Krishna Bharathi
All Rights Reserved.

Dedicated to my family

Contents

Contents

Preface

Hi, friends. I hope that your day went better than yesterday and that you're in the perfect mood to read my book now. Before getting into the plot, I would like to introduce myself to you. I am S. A. Krishna Bharathi, an unstoppable aspirant pursuing my graduation in B. A. Sociology and B. A. Political Science respectively. I am also preparing for the annual civil service examination conducted by the Union Public Service Commission with true passion and dedication. To focus my complete attention on preparation. I wanted to indulge myself in a hobby that would boost my productivity. Hence, after completing this project, I will make sure that I am going to start a full-fledged preparation for my examination. And now, I am bringing my creation before you. Whenever I thought of publishing my book, I never thought about the content that was going to be within it. After a wide range of thoughts and ideas, I finalised my decision to write a book that would inspire people of my age. I don't have enough experience to go beyond that. I also went through enough preparation to get myself ready to write my book. This book is my experience of knowledge that I wanted to share with all the young adolescents in the country. It took me a wide range of research and drafts to finalise the text for this book. Thus, I submit my work to you.

Dad, I Love You!

There are 7 billion individuals on the planet, yet I am fortunate to have you as my father. You are the greatest father of all time. You are my best buddy, my stress reliever, and my ideal father. You are a wonderful human being before you are a great father. You are a fantastic person because of your honesty, truthfulness, helpfulness, nobility, and other positive attributes. I'm at a loss for words when it comes to expressing my feelings for you. Your significance in my life cannot be adequately stated in words. I'm dumbfounded after thinking about your influence on my life. With a smile on your face, you make all the sacrifices. Thank you for always being there for our family and me. Thank you for bringing me into this world. Thank you for always being concerned and lavishing me with love. Thank you for separating the good from the bad for me. Thank you for all of your suggestions and for always giving your support. Thank you for always treating me like a prince, no matter how old I become. Perhaps these thanks come across as a little trite. Dad, I adore you with all of my heart. You are the only person in this universe who is deserving of this love. Whatever I do, wherever I go in life, I will always be grateful to you, Dad, because I know that my existence would be meaningless without you. I'm eternally grateful to the Almighty God for bestowing upon me a parent like you. Thank you so much for what you've done. I adore you to the moon and back.

Mom, I Love You!

You are unlike any other mother in that you gave me life, nurtured me, and were always the first person I called for guidance or simply to say hi. When I fell and sobbed, you were always there to kiss my tears away. You switch on the light for me even though I'm sitting in the dark. It is because of you that I am stronger. You're lovely and delicate around the edges, but you're tough as nails, and I'll be eternally happy that you're mine. There aren't enough words to express how essential you are in my life. I never took the time to tell you how much I appreciate you and everything you've done for me. For all of the times I didn't say thank you because I assumed you know Mom, I thank you now more than ever. Mom, I'd like to express my gratitude for your unending affection. Thank you for being the first place in my heart. The hands that initially held me are still the hands that hold me when I feel lost, and I shall be eternally thankful to you. I'm sorry for any stress I've ever caused you, but I've learned from my errors, and you still helped me get through it. I am very grateful that God chose you to be my mother. Thank you for always being there for me and putting love into all you do. I appreciate and adore you for all of your love, friendship, and support.

Sister, I Love You!

You are my lucky charm. You're my sister, and you're everything to me. You know me better than anybody else, and I have more faith in you than any of my closest friends. All I know is that I am exceedingly privileged to have a down-to-earth and kind sister on whom I can rely and express my ideas. The extent to which you have influenced my life is something I cannot begin to quantify. You are the family's crown jewel, and I adore you. I think about all of the things we've done together since we were kids, and the least I can do is thank you for being such a beautiful sister to me for as long as I can remember. You may not comprehend why or for what reason. But the reality is, I can't picture what life would be like with anybody else as my sister, and I wouldn't want to. All of the memories, laughter, conflicts, pleasures, and sadness pass through my head at all hours of the day and night. I'd do it all over again in a heartbeat if I had to. Please accept my gratitude for being a sister who always makes the effort to be in the right place at the right moment throughout my life. Thank you for being who you are. Thank you for listening when no one else would, and for the friendship we have. Thank you for being a sister who looked out for me when no one else could. Thank you for your wonderful heart, kind temper, and gentle personality, sister.

25 Years Of Love!

Congratulations on your wedding anniversary. Congratulations on your wedding's silver jubilee. Congratulations on attaining a significant milestone built on love and trust. You two became one on this day 25 years ago, travelled a long distance together, and overcame every difficulty with the force of your love. You two demonstrated that, even if life isn't as great as it appears in movies, having a loving partner makes every difficulty worthwhile. After all, you two proved that fairy tales actually exist. You've gotten this far because you've always loved and trusted each other. You were always there for each other in times of sadness and trouble. I witnessed you both many times accepting one another's shortcomings and flaws. If more couples loved like you, love would have a better reputation, and the world would be a better place if more parents were like you. There is nothing more surreal than witnessing a couple like you after 25 years of love, tenderness, and caring. The relationship you two share is incredible and amazing to witness. Only those who are united by divine love can travel such a vast distance and live together. Only excellent spouses can stay together for so many years while raising their children with love and care. You showed us how to live joyfully and patiently in life. Your marriage is a story that will be told for years to come.

Acknowledgements

First and foremost, I thank my family, especially my father, who has always provided me with crucial views that have moulded my philosophy about my writing abilities; my mother, who has always discouraged me from quitting; and my sister, who has always provided me with happy vibes and helped me relax. I would like to thank my friends who were supportive by sharing their views and correcting my errors while writing. I'd want to thank all of the teachers and staff at Reserve Bank Staff Quarters School in Besant Nagar, Chennai and Besant Arundale Senior Secondary School, Kalakshetra Foundation, in Thiruvanmiyur, Chennai for teaching me the fundamentals and assisting in improving my personal skills. I'd also like to express my gratitude to the administrators of both the schools where I studied, as they provided me with the happiest days of my life during my childhood. I'd also like to express my gratitude to the professors of Dwaraka Doss Goverdhan Doss Vaishnav College, in Arumbakkam, Chennai, who provided me with exposure and shared their experiences, allowing me to progress on my way to efforts. I'd want to express my gratitude to Notion Press, my publisher, without whom none of this would have been possible. Finally, I'd like to offer my heartfelt gratitude to the readers who have purchased my book and encouraged me to continue writing. And I'd like to thank the almighty and universal power for providing me with all I asked for, as well as supporting and guiding me through each and every step of my journey to success. I will be remembering everyone till the universe ends.

ACKNOWLEDGEMENTS

Learning Love

When there is harmony in the home,

there is order in the nation.

When there is order in the nation,

there is peace in the world.

I

The Conception

Love is a state of strong attraction towards something. It comprises a wide range of powerful and positive emotional and mental states, from the most virtuous habit to the most basic pleasure or to the deepest interpersonal attachment. It is often observed in both positive and negative states, with its elements expressing kindness, compassion, and affection. It can also refer to acts of compassion and affection for oneself, other individuals, or animals. Love has been proposed as a function that keeps humans together in the face of adversity and helps the survival of the species. Philosophy and religion have provided the greatest speculation on the phenomena of love throughout history. The modern scientific age has recently added to our knowledge of the ideal conception of love.

The psychological degree of identity of two mental representations is referred to as similarity. It underpins our capacity to deal with unfamiliar entities by anticipating how they will behave based on similarities to entities we know. Cognitive psychology research has taken a variety of approaches to the idea of similarity. Each of these is associated with a certain set of knowledge representation assumptions. The degree to which a person's physical traits are aesthetically acceptable or lovely is referred to as physical attractiveness. The phrase is frequently used to refer to sexual appeal or desirability, but it may also refer to something quite else. Both general intellect and physical beauty, according to evolutionary psychologists, may be markers of underlying genetic fitness. The mere-exposure effect is a psychological phenomenon that occurs when people develop a liking for something only because they are familiar with it. This effect is known as the "familiarity principle" in social psychology. Words, Chinese characters, paintings, photographs of people, geometric shapes, and noises have all been used to show the effect. According to research on interpersonal attraction, the more frequently someone sees a person, the more attractive and likeable that person is. John Alan Lee, a Canadian psychologist, developed the colour wheel theory of love. It was initially mentioned in his book Colors of Love: An Exploration of Loving Styles (1973). Lee describes three major, three secondary, and nine tertiary love types using the standard colour wheel. Researchers have discovered a genetic foundation for individual differences in Lee's love styles. Robert Sternberg's triangle theory of love describes three components of love, which are passion, intimacy, and decision-making/commitment. Passion is defined as the urges that lead to romance, physical attraction, sexual consummation, and associated phenomena in loving relationships. Intimacy relates to feelings of closeness, connectivity, and bondedness in a loving relationship; it refers to the choice that one loves a specific person in the short term and the commitment to retain that love in the long term. Love has been viewed as a method for encouraging reciprocal parental support of children. It has been proposed that human language evolved as a form of mating signal that permits potential partners to determine reproductive fitness.

II

The Categories

Love is something that every entity in the cosmos has experienced. Although it is ubiquitous, it comes in a variety of dynamic forms that we have yet to decipher. It is via this feeling of understanding that we are able to distinguish between different types of love and develop the ability to keep them alive.

Love is in its purest form as long as it rests with the individual himself. Self-love is the love one has for as it rests with the individual himself. It is the love one has for himself with regard to one's own happiness. For ages, self-love has been the most basic necessity of humanistic life.

Love, at times, becomes reciprocal and affectionate between two people. A friendship is a more powerful sort of interpersonal tie than an affiliation. In some cultures, friendship is limited to a small number of very deep ties; in others, a person may have many friends as well as a more intense bond with one or two people. A friendly connection between two unrelated people of different sexes or genders is referred to as a cross-sex friendship. Cross-sex friendships can also be problematic for those involved if one or both of them has or has ever had romantic feelings for the other. A romantic friendship is an intimate but non-sexual connection between two people. The friend zone is a conceptual location that describes a scenario in which one person in a mutual friendship aspires to engage in a romantic or sexual connection with the other person.

Love at first sight is a personal experience as well as a common trope in literature: a person or character feels an instant, extreme, and ultimately long-lasting romantic attraction towards a stranger upon first seeing that stranger. Puppy love, often known as a crush, is an informal phrase describing sentiments of romantic love that are commonly experienced during infancy and early adolescence. It gets its name from its likeness to the devoted, worshipful adoration that a puppy may feel. Limerence is a mental condition caused by romantic or non-romantic affections for another person, and it often involves obsessive thoughts and fantasies, as well as a desire to develop or maintain a connection with the object of love and have one's feelings returned. Limerence is sometimes characterised as an uncontrollable feeling of great desire.

Romance, often known as romantic love, is a strong attraction or sense of love for another person, as well as the courting activities used by an individual to communicate those sentiments and the resulting emotions. Compassionate love, also known as altruistic love, is love that focuses on the benefit of the other. It is not the same as charity, compassion, or romantic love. Unconditional love is affection that is free of restrictions, or love that is free of constraints. This word is frequently used interchangeably with concepts like pure altruism or total love.

Conjugal love refers to love in a conjugal relationship, that is, in a marriage, because the term conjugal refers to the relationship between married partners. Platonic love is a non-sexual or romantic sort of love. The word is named after the Greek philosopher Plato, despite the fact that the philosopher never used it himself. Plato's concept of Platonic love involves progressing through stages of proximity to knowledge and genuine beauty, from sexual attraction to particular bodies to attraction to souls, and finally, union with the truth.

Unrequited love, often known as one-sided love, refers to love that is not publicly returned or recognised as such by the beloved. The beloved may be unaware of or willfully reject the admirer's profound and pure adoration.

III

The Perspectives

Love is a universal emotion that anybody may experience. Although it is universal, we need to analyse different interpretations and perspectives of love from various societies. However, researching diverse civilizations perspectives on love appears to be more intriguing and knowledgeable.

In Greek, love is a word used to characterise the ancient Greeks largely homoerotic rituals, behaviours, and attitudes. It was a common term for homosexuality and pederasty. The relevance of an ancient Greek paradigm for current LGBT culture has been called into question. In Jewish ethics and religion, love is a vital virtue. Chesed is a Hebrew word that means kindness or love amongst people, and it refers to both people's religious piety toward God and God's benevolence or charity toward humanity. It is commonly used in the Psalms to imply loving compassion, and it is regarded as the cornerstone of many religious rules followed by traditional Jews. In Europe and North America, the free love movement merged concepts recovered from utopian socialism with anarchism and feminism to criticise the Victorian era's hypocritical sexual morality. In New York's Greenwich Village, bohemian feminists and socialists campaigned for both men's and women's self-realization and enjoyment. Women's equality is usually endorsed by major anarchist philosophers. The term free love refers to a social movement that welcomes all types of love. The primary purpose of the movement was to divorce the state from sexual and romantic affairs such as marriage, birth control, and adultery. It said that such difficulties were solely the responsibility of those engaged. The movement originated in the late 1800s but was significantly advanced by hippies in the 1960s.

Yuanfen, or fateful coincidence, is a Chinese concept that describes both fortunate and negative coincidences and possible partnerships. It may also mean destiny, luck as conditioned by one's history, or natural affinity among pals. It is similar to the Buddhist idea of karma, although yuanfen is interactive rather than individual. Ren is a Confucian virtue that denotes the beneficial qualities of a virtuous individual when they are altruistic. Ren is the outer manifestation of Chinese beliefs, demonstrated by a typical adult's protective instincts towards youngsters. Ren was described by Confucius as wishing to be established himself, and attempting likewise to establish others.

Ishq is an Arabic term that means passion. It is also frequently used in other Muslim languages and on the Indian subcontinent. In its most prevalent classical meaning, ishq relates to the uncontrollable desire to possess the beloved, reflecting a defect that the lover must overcome in order to achieve perfection.

In India, love is classified into three sections. Bhakti denotes attachment, involvement, liking for, reverence, faith, love, devotion, and purity in Sanskrit. Mett is a word that signifies benevolence, loving kindness, friendliness, and an active interest in other people. In both religious and secular Hindu and Buddhist literature, the word Kama frequently connotes sensual pleasure, sexual desire, and longing.

Knowing Relations

When there is harmony in the home,

there is order in the nation.

When there is order in the nation,

there is peace in the world.

IV
The Conception

We have already learned about love and its many elements of knowledge. It is now time for us to learn about the relationships that serve as the foundation for us to play with love. A relationship is defined as the sense of love and connection between two individuals. As a result, having a relationship is one of the most essential things in life. Family relationships, friendships, acquaintances, and sexual relationships are all crucial at some point in life. Relationships can be governed by law, tradition, or mutual agreement, and they serve as the foundation for social groupings and society as a whole. Interpersonal relationships flourish as a result of equitable and reciprocal compromise; they emerge in the context of social, cultural, and other forces.

V

The Ingredients

Relationships are delicate and can be shattered at any time. The elements that support the longevity of partnerships can be corrected to prevent the problems and termination of relationships. Any relationship that flowers is a result of desire. Desires portray their objects favourably, as something that looks like it would be nice.

Personal skills are behavioural habits regardless of their thoughts and feelings in a relationship. The capacity to sense, use, comprehend, manage, and handle emotions is referred to as emotional intelligence. People with high emotional intelligence can notice their own emotions as well as those of others, use emotional information to drive their thoughts and conduct, distinguish between various feelings and name them properly, and alter their emotions to adapt to their surroundings. Like personal skills, social skills are any competency that facilitates engagement and communication with others by creating, communicating, and changing social rules and connections in both spoken and nonverbal ways. Persuasion, active listening, delegating, and stewardship are examples of positive interpersonal skills. Every relationship has to be provided with quality time. That refers to how someone actively engages with another person when they are together, regardless of the length of time they are together. The terms "conflict resolution" and "dispute resolution" are sometimes used interchangeably, especially when arbitration and litigation are involved. Negotiation, mediation, mediation-arbitration, and creative peacebuilding are only a few of the approaches and processes for dealing with conflict. The employment of nonviolent resistance methods by conflicted parties in an attempt to achieve an effective resolution might be conceived of as conflict resolution. The ability to know oneself and others is referred to as social intelligence. Social intelligence develops via interaction with others and learning from successes and mistakes in social situations.

Acceptance as a beholder of any relationship is defined as a person's acquiescence to the reality of a situation, acknowledging a process or condition, typically a bad or uncomfortable circumstance, without seeking to modify or resist it. Emotional intimacy supports every relationship by a feeling of closeness to another that allows for the sharing of personal feelings as well as expectations of understanding, validation, and a display of caring. Affection is commonly used to describe an emotion or sort of love that is more than goodwill or friendship. Affection has given rise to a variety of philosophical and psychological fields concerned with emotions, sickness, influence, and states of being. Some compare it to passion since it lacks the sensory aspect. Any relationship is incomplete without respect, which is defined as a favourable sentiment or action expressed toward someone or something regarded as significant or held in high regard.

It expresses respect for good or useful traits. It is also the process of showing care, worry, or attention to someone's needs or feelings. Possessiveness as a facilitator is defined as thoughts or sentiments of insecurity, dread, or concern about a relative lack of possessions or safety. Sympathy is the necessary awareness, comprehension, and response to another living form's misery or need. According to David Hume, this sympathetic concern is motivated by a shift in perspective from one's own to that of another group or individual in need. Similar to sympathy, empathy is the ability to comprehend or experience what another person is going through from inside their own frame of reference, or to put oneself in another's shoes. Empathy is defined as a wide variety of social, cognitive, and emotional processes that are primarily concerned with understanding others.

VI

The Categories

As relationships are reproductive in nature, they may grow indefinitely. In terms of nomenclature, there are different ways to relate to people. We may observe the relative characteristics of connections here.

A home is the fundamental unit of study in many social, microeconomic, and political models, and it is crucial in economics and inheritance. In human civilization, a family is a group of people who are linked to one another by consanguinity or affinity. The goal of families is to ensure the well-being of their members as well as the well-being of society as a whole.

In sociology, a peer group is a social group as well as a basic group of people who have common interests. Members of this group are likely to have an impact on the person's views and behaviour.

An intimate connection is a type of interpersonal interaction characterised by physical or emotional closeness. Romantic love, sexual intercourse, or other strong attachments define physical intimacy. Emotional intimacy is characterised by sentiments of liking or loving one or more people, and it can lead to physical closeness. These interactions are essential to the human experience.

Any social group is made up of two or more people who interact with one another, have similar qualities, and have a strong feeling of togetherness. It reduces intensive engagement and is based on official rules and procedures rather than personal relationships. A community is a social unit that shares characteristics like norms, religion, beliefs, practises, or identity. Through communication platforms, communities can share a sense of location in a geographical region or in virtual space. An organisation is a social group that distributes responsibilities to achieve a common purpose. A membership in an organisation is a technique that allows people or entities to subscribe. Membership organisations often serve a specific purpose, such as bringing individuals together around a common hobby, geographical region, industry, activity, interest, mission, or profession.

A professional relationship is an interpersonal connection formed by two or more people in a business setting. Professional ties are often more formal than personal relationships. Mentorship is defined as a mentor's influence, advice, or direction provided to a less experienced and frequently younger individual. A mentor impacts a mentee's personal and professional growth in an organisational environment.

An adversary or foe is a person or thing that is thought to be obnoxious or dangerous. The term enemy has the social function of identifying a certain entity as a danger. A frenemy is someone who combines the traits of a friend and an enemy. The phrase refers to personal, geopolitical, and commercial interactions that exist between individuals as well as groups or institutions. This word can also refer to a competitive friendship.

౫

VII
The Activities

There are an endless number of relationships, but they are frequently controlled by abstract and concrete activities. These activities, both directly and indirectly, impact the relationship's uncontrolled stability.

Any relationship that begins with a sense of tremendous excitement or compelling desire for someone or something is referred to as a "passion. Passion can range from fervent interest in or enthusiasm for an idea, proposition, or cause to ecstatic enjoyment of a hobby or pastime. Continuous passion results in the formation of a close, interpersonal relationship between two or more individuals, which is referred to as bonding. It most typically occurs amongst family members or friends, but it may also occur among groups, such as sports teams, or wherever individuals spend time together. Bonding differs from simple like in that it is a mutual, participatory process.

Dating is a stage in which two individuals meet socially with the goal of determining whether or not they are suitable for personal relationships. Dating procedures and practises, as well as the names used to describe them, vary across time. People can date via the phone or internet, or they can meet in person. Some cultures forbid or encourage people to date until they reach a specific age. The period between a marriage proposal and the marriage itself is known as an engagement. A pair is considered to be fiances, or engaged, during this time. The length of the court varies greatly and is mostly determined by cultural standards or the individuals involved consent. Courtship is the period between a man and a woman during which they get to know each other culturally. It is generally preceded by a proposal, commences after a betrothal, and concludes with a marriage celebration. A courtship can be a private event between two people, a public affair, or a formal arrangement with family consent. In the case of a formal engagement, it is the male's responsibility to aggressively court a female, urging her to comprehend him and her openness to a marriage proposal.

Relationships are built only on love and respect. Relationships may, however, be terminated in a number of ways. A break-up is less likely to be used in the context of a married relationship, where a split is usually referred to as a separation or divorce. Some claim that because dating and cohabiting relationships are less socially acknowledged, they might be as unpleasant as or more painful than divorce. When couples in a marriage quit living together but do not divorce, this is referred to as marital separation. A separation can be started informally, or it can be formalised with a separation agreement. In the case of a divorce, the latter may include terms for alimony, whether the children would have exclusive custody or joint custody, and the amount of child support.

ॐ

VIII

The Difficulties

Relationships are divine and unadulterated. However, various things altered the connections and caused issues within them.

When people breach implicit or explicit relationship rules, this is referred to as a relational transgression. It may be a very unpleasant procedure to address relational sins. Repair tactics have the potential to alter a relationship.

The most common form is stalking, the unwanted and repetitive observation of another person by an individual or group. Stalking actions are connected to harassment and intimidation and may include following or monitoring the victim in person. In psychiatry and psychology, the term stalking is used with varying definitions, as well as in certain legal jurisdictions as a term for a criminal act.

Dating abuse or dating violence is defined as the commission or threat of an act of violence by at least one unmarried couple against the other member. Sexual assault, sexual harassment, threats, physical violence, verbal, mental, and emotional abuse, social sabotage, and stalking are all examples.

The phrase hypergamy refers to the habit of women marrying up while men marry down. The antonym hypogamy refers to the opposite, marrying someone from a lower social level or rank.

Sexual repression is a condition in which a person is unable to express their sexuality. Sexual repression manifests itself differently in different cultures, religious communities, and moral systems. Sexual suppression can be classified as either physical, mental, or a combination of the two. Infidelity is a breach of the emotional and sexual exclusivity of a relationship. Both men and women may face societal repercussions if an act of adultery is made public.

An abusive person frequently uses abusive power and control to obtain and keep dominance. The abuser may be motivated by a multitude of factors, including devaluation, jealousy, personal gain, personal fulfilment, psychological projection, or just the thrill of wielding power.

Domestic violence can manifest itself in a variety of ways, including physical, verbal, emotional, financial, religious, reproductive, or sexual abuse. Domestic murder can take the form of stoning, bride burning, honour killing, or dowry death. Women are more likely than men to use intimate relationship violence as a form of self-defense. Domestic violence is one of the most underreported crimes in the world, affecting both men and women. Abuse can result in a violent intergenerational cycle in children and other family members. Many people might not see themselves as abusers or victims because they may view their experiences as out-of-control family conflicts.

Physical, sexual, and psychological mistreatment or neglect of a child by a parent or caregiver is referred to as child abuse or child maltreatment. Various jurisdictions have evolved their own views on obligatory reporting as well as different definitions of what constitutes child abuse for the purpose of removing children from their homes or prosecuting a criminal prosecution. A narcissistic parent is one who has narcissism or a narcissistic personality disorder. Narcissists have poor self-esteem and feel the urge to exert control over how others perceive them. They are also rigid and lack the empathy required for child rearing. Personal boundaries are frequently crossed in order to shape and manipulate the child.

Elder abuse is defined as a single or recurrent act that occurs in any relationship where there is an expectation of trust and causes injury or distress to an older person. Because many kinds of elder abuse are done by family members, they are classified as forms of domestic violence or family violence. Paid carers have been accused of preying on their elderly charges.

Loving Professionally

When there is harmony in the home,

there is order in the nation.

When there is order in the nation,

there is peace in the world.

IX

The Explanation

Man is a social animal. He can't survive on his own, so he needs the companionship of others. We have been on this planet for about a million years and have witnessed numerous changes in our civilization. Despite the fact that we have advanced to the point where we can call ourselves civilized, there are growing inequalities and conflicts in many aspects of man's existence. To get right to the issue, we need to figure out what is causing all of these problems for the human species. There is an enormous quantity of scientific evidence demonstrating that we, as humans, rely on one another for nourishment and life. So, what is the true issue in terms of the human condition? It is man himself who consistently refuses to contribute to himself and society and instead complains about the errors of others! So, while a small portion of the total population is willing to address current issues, they are requesting the key solution, which is a change of heart! So this is just a basic proposal by myself. That is love, which is the only remedy and the lone weapon for changing the world's inequalities and conflicts. To give and receive love, one must first comprehend the broad notion of love and relationships in order to comprehend the perfect form of the concept and maybe become an expert in it by becoming a professional lover. Only a professional lover can survive in today's changing world. A professional lover is someone who utilises love as their primary weapon in order to win the fight against him. He never lost in his battle, just as love never did.

X

The Significance

So far, we've covered a lot of ground when it comes to love and relationships, and you should have a good understanding of them by now. So we must now be aware of how to apply this essential knowledge appropriately. As said at the outset, there must be the arrival of a professional lover who may be a growing answer to all of the world's disputes and inequalities. To begin with, love must be viewed as a profession with certain do's and don'ts that must be strictly adhered to. A profession is something you know how to do well. To begin a profession, you must first understand the principles and fundamentals of that field. Consideration of love as a career provides it with more definite shape and helps a person to better expose and display their beautiful craftsmanship. A professional lover is someone who utilises love as their primary weapon to triumph despite all odds. To be a professional lover, one must be aware of all the considerations that must be made. You will be aware of all of the unique notes and points regarding how to become a professional lover.

XI
Preparing Love

Love is not only words or physical contact, despite what some people may believe. Love is a biochemical phenomenon that alters your behaviour subtly as well as physically. Being in love is wonderful, life-changing, fantastic, and incredibly difficult.

Love is a feeling that comes easily and without any effort. Love is a tough concept to define. The search for love might appear to go on forever since it is so elusive. You must first comprehend the meaning of love in order to be able to really love someone. Every day, there are references to love, but defining what it actually means can be challenging. People have varied definitions of what love is, and depending on the circumstance, you might feel different kinds of love. We know it exists because others have it, yet the road may be so difficult to navigate that it might be tempting to give up.

There are many distinct types of love, and there is no one way to tell if you are truly experiencing one or merely going through a major case of infatuation. Whether you're in love or infatuated, it's important to be honest with yourself about your feelings. If this describes your current situation, you could find it difficult to control your emotions. You could be looking for strategies to deal with the rush of so many new emotions you're feeling.

Fortunately, there are several adjustments you can make right away to increase your chances of finding love. Even though it seems difficult, finding true love that fulfils you is easier to achieve than you might imagine. If you look for suitable partners, create a fulfilling connection, and focus on developing deep love with that person, you can find unconditional love.

XII

Expressing Love

Love is not as straightforward as it is frequently depicted in the media. Being able to love someone the way you want to is a skill that takes practice, just like any other skill. There are various ways you can work on loving and expressing your love. Learning your preferred method of expressing love is important since everyone has their own unique preferences. Receiving gifts, quality time, words of affirmation, acts of service, and physical touch are the five love languages. Being in a relationship of any kind requires you to be aware of your love language.

It's important to love yourself as much as you can, even if at times it may seem easier to love others than oneself. The development of good relationships with others depends in large part on one's ability to embrace oneself. Recognizing your own value and leading your life honestly are both examples of loving oneself. There are many things you can do to improve your attitude, regardless of your situation. You'll soon be leading a happier, more loving existence if you silence your inner, critical voice and focus more on the positive things and people in your life. You must put equal effort into encouraging kindness and peace in the world as well as discovering love and peace inside yourself. Doing this can be challenging, particularly when life is challenging, tough, and unbelievably busy. However, setting peace, love, and happiness as your top priorities can help you to prioritise things clearly, declutter your thoughts, and take the right route in life. Luckily, you can learn to do this with a little effort and perseverance. Looking on the bright side often requires conscious effort if you want to be pleased with your life. Being optimistic and constructive can help you become a more loving person.

You should be able to tell whether you're truly in love if you pay attention to your actions and feelings around your special someone. You may feel anxious about telling someone you love them, but you'll feel so much better once you do. Fortunately, by identifying the source of your hesitation, you can process your feelings and reopen your heart to love.

To truly love the people you care about, you must engage with them, be honest with them, and forgive those who have wronged you. To truly love your partner, you must establish a close relationship with him and put their needs first. It's crucial to express your emotions to your loved one in a way that they will understand and value if you want to keep a loving connection. Simple actions like grinning, asking for assistance, and being adaptable may make a lot of people fall in love with you.

It might be challenging to find yourself in a relationship when the love is one-sided. To show your partner that you care in both new and traditional ways, utilise your words, your deeds, your touch, and your presents.

Just remember that you can't make someone love you. There is no foolproof method for making love happen because it is a complex mixture of factors, including circumstances and chemistry. All you can do is try to set up the ideal environment and wait for the results. Although you can't make someone do anything, you may inspire or persuade them with your appeal.

XIII
Accepting Love

One of life's most romantic moments is falling in love, but the concept of love is so ambiguous. There are ways to enjoy and be appreciative of your job rather than despise it.

Love may mean different things to different people, and there is no way to know if someone really loves you or if they just have a crush on you. It could be possible to love several people and still be realistic if it means accepting and respecting others. It definitely doesn't include agreeing with or loving everyone, but you may try your best to uphold each person's dignity.

At first, it may seem difficult to love someone who loves you, but there are ways to let your heart open up. Work on accepting and embracing love once you've discovered the perfect person and are prepared for it. Step back and consider your relationship impartially. This is the best way to determine whether you're in love or not. Consider how you behave around this individual once you've identified how they affect your feelings. It isn't always easy to see the admirable traits of the individuals standing right in front of us. You can reach a point of love and acceptance if you take the time to get to know the other person better, let go of expectations and perfection, sympathise with them, and express gratitude to them. Even though you might want to adore that person, it could be challenging to accept and love them for who they are.

If you want to determine whether the person you love actually loves you, you must pay attention to how they act, speak, and behave when you are together.

XIV

Persevering Love

Being in love and remaining in love are both stages of the relationship process. Love isn't always a black and white situation, and when you're in the middle of a grey region, it can be challenging to understand your emotions. There are certain emotions that are present in all forms of love, even though what being in love means will vary from person to person.

Many individuals put a lot of effort into finding a long-term partner, but they aren't sure how to keep the romance alive after it's established. You might be curious about how a relationship will develop and how to show that you care while you're in one. You may cooperate in a variety of ways to maintain the romance in your union and make it last for a very long time.

It may be challenging to be In a long-distance relationship, particularly when it comes to communication. Focusing on the love and happiness you feel for your partner can frequently be hindered by the realities of life. Your love for your partner should be established first, but even that may be difficult to say when you are apart from them. Being optimistic and having constructive conversations are essential to growing in love. Being truthful and allowing yourself to open up in a phone conversation, video chat, or even text message will benefit your relationship. By creating intimacy and an emotional bond, you might be able to pave the way for love if you're determined. If you are prepared to put in the time and effort, you can relive those emotions. With a little more effort, you can show your love and keep your relationship going strong.

XV
Concluding Love

When two people fall in love, they may live happily ever after. When love fails, at least one person might suffer harm. There are many reasons why relationships end. Sometimes the end is permanent, and occasionally it isn't. There may come a point when you just don't want to fall in love. Various strategies may be used to overcome your fear of being loved.

If your romantic relationship is a one-way street, you probably fell in love with the wrong person at the wrong moment. When someone you love doesn't return your affection, it's quite acceptable to feel sad, frustrated, and a little lost. When someone you love doesn't reciprocate your feelings, it might seem as though the world is coming to an end. The idea that no one loves you in life may be a harsh, empty feeling. Even rejection affects the same pain-sensing neurons in your brain as physical pain does.

Some people choose to never fall in love again because of the wounds from past relationships. However, due to misunderstandings or poor communication, you might not be aware of how much you are truly loved.

If you are unsure if you are still in love with your partner, you might be able to tell by looking at changes in your relationship. If you're struggling with feelings for someone who is off-limits, not a good fit for you, or entered your life at a bad time, take some time to think about how you might feel about them. By looking at the amount of attraction and physicality, communication patterns, and bad relationship patterns, you can determine if your relationship needs some work or whether you are actually losing interest.

It might be hard to move on after being harmed by a loved one. Although it can seem like the wisest course of action to change your love into hatred, doing so would simply make things more difficult for you.

It takes determination and perseverance to learn how to not fall in love, especially when you feel like you can't control your feelings. To prevent your feelings from controlling you, you might try ignoring the person you are attracted to and emotionally cutting off from them. You can pinpoint the causes of your anxiety, deal with unfavourable thoughts, and talk to a friend or partner.

As a means of separating yourself from someone you could be falling for, you can also concentrate on your own requirements and interests. The greatest thing you can do is cope with your feelings and concentrate on moving forward in life. Try to find your own fulfilment in life and keep a distance from the person you have feelings for. You can enjoy being single and be happy if you process your feelings and take care of your needs. Decide what love means to you and move on.

It's common for people to develop romantic feelings for fictional characters they've encountered in a book, movie, television show, or video game. You should take care to ensure that these love feelings don't interfere with your ability to lead a normal life. By recognising that by managing your emotions and seeking out healing, you can help yourself.

There is no assurance that your relationship can be saved after adultery. But it will take time, a lot of work, and sacrifice to express your regret and dedication to forging a better relationship going forward.

When a loved one takes their own life, you might need coping mechanisms to help you understand your feelings and take care of yourself. All of us have experienced death at least once. It's never easy to lose a loved one. Learning to function without them might be daunting since grief is a tricky feeling. It can be challenging to know what to do to help or comfort someone you know who has lost a loved one. There are ways for you to continue enjoying your life while still honouring your loved one and being fully present in the world of the living. Even though it's difficult, you can figure out how to rebuild your life without your loved one.

Examining your motivations in depth will give you the strength to end your relationship with love. By putting distance between you, dealing with your pain, and continuing with your life, you may stop loving someone.

XVI

Mastering Love

To begin with the most fundamental concept, love is a universal, pure, and abstract emotion. Everyone understands, categorises, proves, and follows it in their own unique way. Although everyone is aware of love and relationships since they have been witnessing them since infancy, there are numerous disputes and inequities that would fill a million pages if they were enumerated. The situation has deteriorated to the point that people are opposing themselves. Animals do not exhibit this type of behaviour. Even if a prey item passes by, if the animal is not hungry, it will not hunt it down. But, because of our great greed and uncontrollable need, we tend to accumulate a lot of ephemeral money while leaving all the permanent love behind. Everyone who has known us since childhood knows that we only have one life. It is also certain that everyone who was born on this piece of land will die one day. Despite all the obstacles, one should give and pour love on others in order to receive everything back one day. It would be whenever there is a pandemic, war, or other external damage. Whatever we may gain materially will fade and abandon us one day. The kindness and respect we provide others will be returned to us one day. At their essence, all sacred writings from all civilizations say the same thing. A professional lover, as described in this book, will live his life to the fullest, even if he is a total failure in material matters. Only a professional lover will be able to survive and thrive in the future. And this is the true idea of transferring the concept of professional love to our ever-changing modern world with its numerous conditions. The ultimate goal of the professional lover is to give and to be loved.

BIBLIOGRAPHY

Definition of LOVE. (1987, December 27). Love Definition & Meaning - Merriam-Webster. Retrieved October 9, 2022, from https://www.merriam-webster.com/dictionary/love

Definition of love | Dictionary.com. (n.d.). www.dictionary.com. Retrieved October 9, 2022, from https://www.dictionary.com/browse/love

Is Love Biological or Is It a Cultural Phenomenon? (2022, July 17). Verywell Mind. Retrieved October 9, 2022, from https://www.verywellmind.com/what-is-love-2795343

Fresh, F. (2020, January 17). The 8 Different Types of Love + the Perfect Combo for You | FTD. FTD.com. Retrieved October 9, 2022, from https://www.ftd.com/blog/give/types-of-love

Learn the Different Types of Love (and Better Understand Your Partner) - Lifehack. (2018, November 16). Lifehack. Retrieved October 9, 2022, from https://www.lifehack.org/816195/types-of-love

8 Types Of Love + How To Find Out Which One You Have | mindbodygreen. (n.d.). 8 Types of Love + How to Find Out Which One You Have | Mindbodygreen. Retrieved October 9, 2022, from https://www.mindbodygreen.com/articles/types-of-love

Expressions of love displayed in different cultures | News | dailytitan.com. (2005, February 7). Daily Titan. Retrieved October 9, 2022, from https://dailytitan.com/news/expressions-of-love-displayed-in-different-cultures/article_37cd7cef-8528-56ff-b285-81c6a01073e8.html

Hofmann, L. (2020, October 9). Love Around the World: different countries, different preferences - TheCurvyMagazine. TheCurvyMagazine. Retrieved October 9, 2022, from https://thecurvymagazine.com/en/fashion/love-around-the-

world-different-countries-different-preferences

A. (2020, July 15). "Love" in different languages. App2Brain. Retrieved October 9, 2022, from https://app2brain.com/learn-languages/words-phrases/love/

Definition of RELATIONSHIP. (2022, September 29). Relationship Definition & Meaning - Merriam-Webster. Retrieved October 9, 2022, from https://www.merriam-webster.com/dictionary/relationship

relationship. (2022, October 5). RELATIONSHIP | Definition in the Cambridge English Dictionary. Retrieved October 9, 2022, from https://dictionary.cambridge.org/us/dictionary/english/relationship

C. (2020, September 15). 12 elements of healthy relationships - Johns Hopkins University Student Well-Being. Johns Hopkins University Student Well-Being. Retrieved October 9, 2022, from https://wellbeing.jhu.edu/blog/2020/09/15/12-elements-of-healthy-relationships/

Characteristics of Healthy & Unhealthy Relationships | Youth.gov. (n.d.). Characteristics of Healthy & Unhealthy Relationships | Youth.gov. Retrieved October 9, 2022, from https://youth.gov/youth-topics/teen-dating-violence/characteristics

8 Elements of a Healthy Relationship | Psychology Today. (2022, September 1). Psychology Today. Retrieved October 9, 2022, from https://www.psychologytoday.com/us/blog/invisible-bruises/202208/8-elements-healthy-relationship

What Type Of Relationship Are You In? A Big Glossary Of Dating Terms. (2021, June 12). Mindbodygreen. Retrieved October 9, 2022, from https://www.mindbodygreen.com/articles/types-of-relationships

What Are the Different Types of Relationships? 35 Terms to Know. (n.d.). Healthline. Retrieved October 9, 2022, from https://www.healthline.com/health/types-of-relationships

LovePanky, T. (2021, June 28). 26 Different Types of Relationships to Predict Your Romantic Life & Future. LovePanky - Your Guide to Better Love and Relationships. Retrieved October 9, 2022, from https://www.lovepanky.com/flirting-flings/dating-game/types-of-relationships

Every Relationship Goes Through These 5 Stages: Where Are You? (2020, June 21). Mindbodygreen. Retrieved October 9, 2022, from https://www.mindbodygreen.com/articles/stages-of-a-relationship

How to Successfully Crack the Code of Love. (2022, August 29). Verywell Mind. Retrieved October 9, 2022, from https://www.verywellmind.com/the-four-stages-of-relationships-4163472

Muzik, B. (2012, December 3). The 5 Relationship Stages. Relationship & Marriage Advice. Retrieved October 9, 2022, from https://www.loveatfirstfight.com/relationship-advice/relationship-stages/

PsyD., LPC, M. R. (2022, January 4). 15 Most Common Relationship Problems & Solutions — Talkspace. Talkspace. Retrieved October 9, 2022, from https://www.talkspace.com/blog/relationship-problems/

30 Common Relationship Problems and Solutions. (2017, June 8). Marriage Advice - Expert Marriage Tips & Advice. Retrieved October 9, 2022, from https://www.marriage.com/advice/relationship/solutions-for-8-common-relationship-issues/

Signs of Serious Relationship Problems | Psychology Today. (2022, September 1). Psychology Today. Retrieved October 9, 2022, from https://www.psychologytoday.com/us/blog/toxic-relationships/201904/signs-serious-relationship-problems